Voyager 1 & 2

by Bob Italia

Published by Abdo & Daughters, 6535 Cecilia Circle, Bloomington, Minnesota 55435

Library bound edition distributed by Rockbottom Books, Pentagon Tower, P.O. Box 36036, Minneapolis, Minnesota 55435

Library of Congress Number: 90-082622   ISBN: 0-939179-96-2

Cover Photo by: NASA Jet Propulsion Laboratory
Inside Photos by: Bettmann Newsphotos

Edited by Rosemary Wallner

— Contents —

How it all Began

In the mid-1960s, scientists at the Jet Propulsion Laboratory (JPL) in Pasaedena, California, began to prepare for the next decade of space exploration. A wonderful opportunity to tour the outer planets of the solar system would be coming up during the last half of the 1970s. Jupiter, Saturn, Uranus, Neptune, and Pluto would align on the same side of the sun. These planets had not been aligned this way in over a hundred years. And they would not align again until the year 2159.

Astronomers had many questions about the outer planets. What was the great Red Spot on Jupiter made of? What made up the smaller white ovals on that giant planet? What were Saturn's rings made of? Did Titan, Saturn's largest moon, have an atmosphere? A journey to the outer planets would answer these questions. Preparations for the journey began at once.

*Instruction in the revolution of the planets to
19th Century schoolchildren.*

But before scientists could receive any money to build a spacecraft to explore the outer planets, they had to figure out how the unmanned spacecraft would be powered. The outer planets were too far away from the sun, so the spacecraft could not be run on solar power.

The nuclear industry provided the answer. Plutonium, which gives off heat, could be put in a thermoelectric converter. This converter would change heat into electrical energy and power the spacecraft for years.

Once that problem was solved, a proposal to tour the outer planets—called the Grand Tour—was given to the National Aeronautics and Space Administration (NASA) for approval. The scientists proposed the construction of two spacecraft that would fly to Jupiter, Saturn, Uranus, and Neptune beginning in 1977. NASA presented the plan to Congress for final approval. This space mission, initially called Mariner Jupiter Saturn, would cost American taxpayers millions of dollars. Only Congress could approve the plan and provide the needed funds. After much debate, Congress approved the mission. Now it was time to turn the plans into reality.

A launch date in 1977 was set. If the deadline was missed, the mission could not be performed.

Before building the spacecraft, scientists had to decide what they wanted to investigate once the spacecraft arrived at the planets. Because the spacecraft would be flying past the planets at incredible speeds, only a few hours could be spent investigating each planet. Scientists had to decide which scientific instruments would best record the images of the planets.

Many instruments would be needed. A radio system would be used to transmit and receive information. Television cameras would be used to take photographs. Other instruments would be used to analyze light, cosmic rays, magnetic fields, and radio waves given off by each planet. Finally, scientists decided on all the instruments that would be needed.

But what would the spacecraft look like?

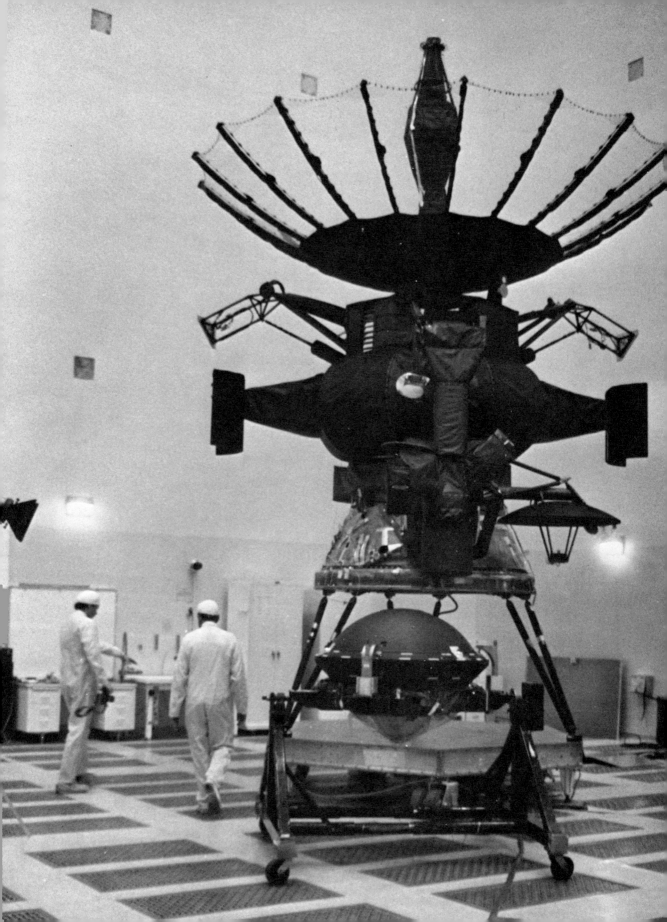

Robot Voyagers

Engineers at the JPL worked on the design of the spacecraft that would carry all the instruments to the outer planets. The designers had a difficult job. Little was known about the dangers of space beyond Jupiter. The spacecraft had to be just the right size and weight or it would not fit onto a rocket. If it could not fit, it could not leave the launching pad. The spacecraft had to be completed one year before the launch. Scientists would need that year to make final checks.

After many years of planning and building, two spacecraft, now named *Voyager 1* and *Voyager 2,* were completed. (The old name of Mariner Jupiter Saturn was dropped.) Each of these semi-intelligent robots weighed nearly a ton and were large enough to fit into a garage. Each had three separate computers, a small nuclear power plant, two television cameras, and a radio transmitter. The transmitter ran on only twenty-two watts, yet was capable of beaming images across 3.5 billion miles of space.

Voyager being built and tested.

While engineers had been constructing the spacecraft, the Mission Design Team (MDT) had been choosing flight paths for each of the spacecraft. *Voyager 1* would travel very close to Jupiter, then fly on to Saturn for a close look at its moon Titan. *Voyager 2* would not fly as close to Jupiter but would investigate the planet's moons. The MDT had to use a computer to pick the best two flight plans out of a possible 12,000 flight plans.

The Launch

When everything was ready, each *Voyager* spacecraft was placed on its own Titan-Centaur launch vehicle (rocket). Then each spacecraft's computer was supplied with hundreds of instructions.

Launching Voyager into space on a
Titan-Centaur rocket.

With a brilliant burst of light and energy, *Voyager 2* was launched on August 20, 1977. *Voyager 2* had a later arrival date at Jupiter than *Voyager 1*, so it was launched first. Minutes later, serious problems arose. The spacecraft had vibrated violently when it had left the ground. It had started to spin rapidly when it separated from the launch vehicle. No one knew why. If the spinning could not be stopped, *Voyager 2* would destroy itself.

Hours passed before *Voyager 2* began responding to new commands sent from Mission Control on Earth. Soon, the spacecraft was stabilizing and out of danger. Now it could continue its voyage through space to Jupiter.

The launching of *Voyager 1* was next. September 5, 1977, was selected as its lift-off date. For the first few minutes, the launch went as planned. But then *Voyager 1* ran into trouble.

The Titan rocket shut down too early. That meant the Centaur rocket had to burn longer than planned to make up for Titan's short-comings. Would there be enough fuel in the Centaur rocket to accomplish this feat? No one knew for sure.

The fuel in the Centaur rocket lasted just long enough for *Voyager 1* to detach itself on time. Five seconds more, and Centaur would have run out of fuel. But it did not matter. Everything was running smoothly again. *Voyager 1* was on its way to Jupiter. On Day 13 of its mission, *Voyager 1* took a photograph of Earth and Moon together. It was the first time that a photo of our planet and its moon had been taken.

Voyager 1 and *2* Reach Jupiter

Jupiter is the fifth planet from the sun. It is the largest planet, measuring nearly 280,000 miles around its equator (center). Like most of the outer planets, it is composed of gases. Jupiter is nearly 400 million miles from Earth.

By December 15, 1977, both *Voyager* space-crafts were 78 million miles away from Earth. *Voyager 1* had a shorter flight path and more speed, so it had already passed *Voyager 2*. On Day 207, *Voyager 2*'s main transmitter failed. Luckily, the spacecraft's backup transmitter was activated.

In 1978, the *Voyager* spacecraft spent nine months passing through the dangerous asteroid belt between Mars and Jupiter. No one knew if the spacecraft would be hit by an asteroid. The scientists monitoring the craft watched and waited. Finally, both *Voyagers* made it through without any problems. Perhaps, the scientists said, the asteroid belt was not as dangerous as they had first thought.

When *Voyager 1* was eighty days away from Jupiter, a series of computer commands began to prepare the craft for its encounter with the huge planet. Soon *Voyager 1* would be taking photos of Jupiter and sending them 400 million miles back to Earth. Preparations had to be made at this point. Because of the tremendous distances involved, it took a long time for radio commands to reach the spacecraft.

In December 1978, the first photos of Jupiter arrived at the JPL. The photos were interesting, but nothing like they would be when *Voyager 1* drew nearer to the big planet. When it did, the photos became breathtaking.

By studying the photos, scientist could see that Jupiter was not a stable planet. The clouds of Jupiter were always moving, always swirling. Spots appeared, then disappeared. Scientists discovered that the bands of brilliant golds, reds, pinks, and blues that covered the planet were gaseous jet streams.

Voyager 1 was now streaking towards Jupiter, traveling 600,000 miles per day. The photos it took became more spectacular and more brilliant. But the scientists at the JPL still had concerns. What would happen when the tiny *Voyager 1* reached Jupiter's immense and powerful radiation field? Would *Voyager 1* burn up? Would its instruments be destroyed? By March 2, 1979, the scientists had their answer. Despite the intense radiation, *Voyager 1* was ready and alert for its close encounter with Jupiter.

A dramatic view of Jupiter's Great Red Spot
and its surroundings taken by Voyager.

And then suddenly, there it was—Jupiter's Great Red Spot seen as it had never been seen before. The Great Red Spot is a giant storm, like a hurricane. The storm is as large as six Earths. People at the JPL were able to watch the great red storm churning and swirling as if the planet were right outside. Then on March 4, *Voyager 1*, traveling at 84,000 miles an hour, came within 173,000 miles of the planet. It took as many pictures as it could as it curved around Jupiter and its many moons. *Voyager 1* was then maneuvered so it could examine Jupiter's dark side.

After its examination of Jupiter, *Voyager 1* hurled itself into the darkness of space, now traveling at 50,000 miles an hour. The craft sped towards Saturn, 500 million miles away.

On July 6, 1979, *Voyager 2* reached Jupiter's radiation field. It passed within 134,000 miles of Europa, one of Jupiter's moons, and within 40,000 miles of Ganymede, another moon. The craft passed a third moon, Io, for another close inspection. *Voyager 2* took more photos of the giant planet, then quickly sailed out of Jupiter's radiation field. Voyager 2 now began following *Voyager 1* to Saturn, two years away.

What the *Voyagers* Discovered

Voyager 1 and *2* each had taken 18,000 photographs of Jupiter. The most spectacular photos were published in newspapers and magazines around the world.

Some of the more interesting photographs were of Jupiter's moons. The photos showed that the moon Callisto had an icy crust and was heavily cratered. Ganymede had strange-looking tracks. Europa had thin stripes and cracks that criss-crossed its smooth, craterless surface. And on Io, *Voyager 1* had taken a photo of an erupting volcano—the first active volcano discovered outside of Earth. *Voyager 2* discovered six other active volcanos on Io.

Other photographs were truly amazing. One revealed a ring around Jupiter. The ring was not like Saturn's huge ring system, but it was there, thin and flat and not very clear. *Voyager 2* had

This striking view of Jupiter's ring was recorded by Voyager 2.

taken a dazzling photograph of the newly
discovered ring. The ring's particles had been lit
momentarily by the sun's rays. *Voyager 1* took
beautiful photographs of lightning storms on
Jupiter's dark side.

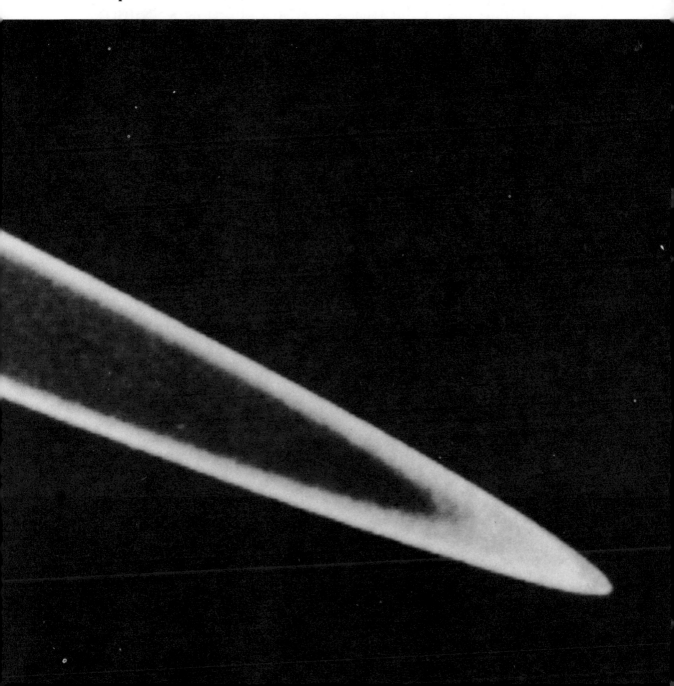

The Saturn Encounter

Saturn is the sixth planet from the sun. It is the second largest planet, measuring 235,000 miles at its equator. Composed of mostly gases, Saturn is famous for its rings. Saturn is nearly 800 million miles from Earth.

In August 1980, *Voyager 1* began to take photos of Saturn. Compared to Jupiter's bands of bright colors, Saturn was dull, composed of a golden haze.

Voyager 1 passed within 2,500 miles of Saturn's giant moon Titan. Titan had an atmosphere similar to Earth's atmosphere. But temperatures on Titan's surface hovered around -289 degrees Fahrenheit.

Voyager 1 made its closest approach to Saturn on November 12. Now the golden haze of the planet seemed to have different color bands. *Voyager 1* clocked Saturn's winds at 1,100 miles an hour. Not even Jupiter's Great Red Spot had winds that violent.

Voyager 1 streaked past and under Saturn's ring system. The system was 87,000 miles wide, and was composed of hundreds of rings. Each ring was made of ice crystals and snowballs. An outer ring, called the F ring, actually consisted of two separate rings twisted together.

Voyager 1 continued to the rest of Saturn's moons. Three new moons were discovered. One moon had a crater that covered a fourth of the moon's entire surface.

Once it was finished inspecting the ringed planet, *Voyager 1* left the solar system. Its mission had been accomplished. It had performed flawlessly. Now it was time to journey into the uncluttered vastness of space that existed between the stars.

Voyager 2 arrived at Saturn in August 1981, nine months after *Voyager 1*. It took a close-up look at Saturn's rings and discovered spokes in the rings. *Voyager 2* traveled to within 63,000 miles of the planet's cloudy surface. The craft photographed a storm,in the shape of the number 6, with winds of nearly 300 miles an hour. *Voyager 2* traveled to the outer moons and took a closer look at the newly discovered ones.

Finally, *Voyager 2* left Saturn. But it would not yet join its sister ship in its journey to oblivion. *Voyager 2* was now headed towards Uranus.

Voyager 2
Reaches Uranus and Neptune

Uranus is the seventh planet from the sun. It is sixty-three times as big as Earth. It is made up of gasses, has many rings and moons, and is 1.7 billion miles from Earth.

In December 1985, four years after it had left Saturn, *Voyager 2* neared the planet Uranus and its moons. The craft flew past Miranda, the smallest moon. Miranda was oval shaped and had canyons twelve miles deep. Scientists think that at one time this moon had been blown up during a violent collision with a meteor, then had somehow put itself together again. Ten other new moons were discovered.

Voyager 2 inspected Uranus's rings and found fifty more. The rings were very slender and blackened with methane.

This photo was taken by Voyager 2. Saturn's icy moons can be seen in the upper left corner (small white spots).

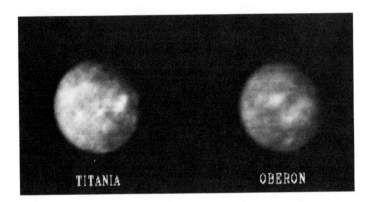

*The five largest moons of Uranus: Miranda,
the smallest of the five; the two largest, Oberon and
Titania, are about half the size of Earth's moon;
Ariel shows the largest contrast on its surface.*

24

During its journeys around Uranus, *Voyager 2* made a strange discovery about Uranus's rotation. Unlike other planets, which rotate on a north/south axis (pole), Uranus rotates on an east/west axis, as if it had been knocked over by something very big and powerful. Perhaps a huge meteorite or comet had struck it.

After its close encounter with Uranus, *Voyager 2* prepared for its last journey. This time the craft would travel to Neptune.

Neptune is the eighth planet from the sun. It is the fourth largest planet, composed of blue gases. It is 2.7 billion miles from Earth.

Not many people thought *Voyager 2* would make it to Neptune. Yet in late August 1989, *Voyager 2* reached the blue planet, and was faithfully reporting back to Earth. *Voyager 2* had now been in space for twelve years.

As it traveled near Neptune, *Voyager 2* discovered six new moons and traces of three thin rings. It also discovered two dark blue spots similar to Jupiter's Great Red Spot. One of the dark blue spots was the size of Earth. It was named the Great Dark Spot, and its winds traveled at 700 miles per hour. *Voyager 2* discovered that the temperature on Neptune was -400 degrees Fahrenheit, and its winds were more powerful than Jupiter's.

Voyager 2 also visited Neptune's most famous moon, Triton. Triton is a beautiful moon. It is a pale rose color. It has volcanos and geysers that gush freezing chemicals. *Voyager 2* discovered that Triton was slowly orbiting closer and closer to Neptune. One day, Neptune will swallow Triton in its blue gases.

Voyager 2 had finally completed its mission. It was time to join its sister ship in the lonely trek into the unknown reaches of space.

Scientist Dr. Edward Stone shows Voyager 2's encounter with Neptune's moon Triton.

Into Deep Space

Voyager 1 and *2* have become our greatest explorers. They have traveled billions of miles and are destined to sail into space forever. In 100,000 years, they will reach the nearest star. A million years after that, they will encounter the next nearest star. Space is extremely vast. Only our robot explorers can survive such a long trip. But by then, *Voyagers'* power plants will have run out of nuclear fuel. Their instruments will have been burned out by billions of years of radiation bombardment. All that will be left of the *Voyagers* will be their lifeless metal shells.

But just in case there are other life forms in other solar systems who might discover the spacecraft, a message has been placed aboard each *Voyager* spacecraft.

Before the *Voyagers* were launched, a gold-plated copper phonograph record was attached to each craft. Near the record is a cartridge, record needle, and instructions on how to operate the record.

The record contains the sounds of music and greetings in fifty-three languages. An ocean surf, human heartbeat, and the cry of a baby are also recorded. On it are the sounds of birds, crickets, elephants, and whales. There is even a message from Jimmy Carter, who was president at the time the *Voyagers* were launched. "This is a present from a small distant world," he says, "a token of our sounds, our images, our thoughts, and our feelings."

Photographs also accompany the *Voyagers*. Some of the photos include people, animals, buildings, and human inventions.

Will anyone, or anything ever see the photographs? Will they ever hear the messages? Perhaps only our greatest explorers, *Voyager 1* and *Voyager 2*, will ever know.

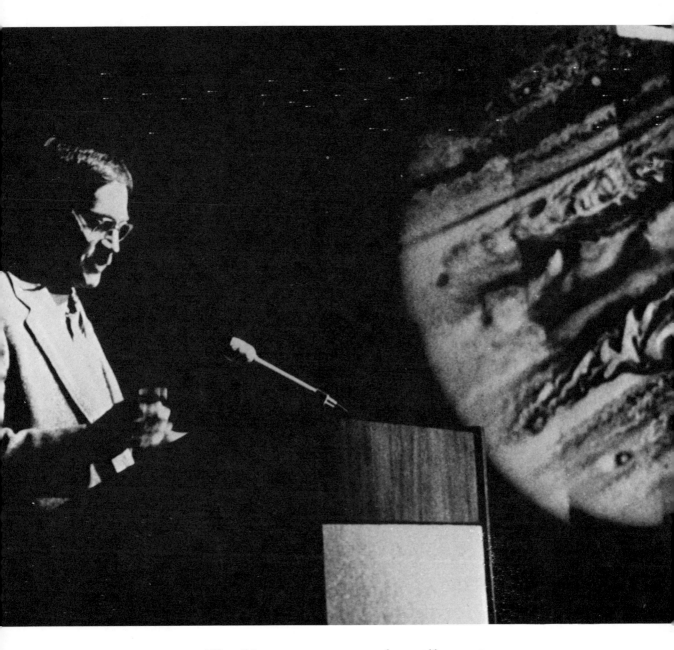

*The Voyager spacecrafts will continue
to relay photographs of our galaxy back to Earth
far into the future.*